BEING USED

by

God

Finding Renewed Purpose in Life's Changing Seasons

A clear guide to help you clarify your purpose and live it out with confidence.

JIM DEAN

BEING
USED
by
God

Being Used by God: Finding Renewed Purpose in Life's Changing Seasons

ISBN: 978-1-966596-26-4 *(paperback)*
978-1-966596-27-1 *(ebook)*

Proofreading, cover design, and formatting services by
ChristianEditingandDesign.com.

Contents

Introduction   7

1. Where Are You Now?   11

2. What Got You Here?   16

3. What If Everything Turned Out As You Hoped?   18

4. Experience a Fulfilling Life of Purpose   23

5. Be Intentional with Your Platforms   26

6. Get Clear About Your Purpose   35

7. Make the Important People in Your Life a Priority   45

8. Harness Your Unique Design for Your Purpose   56

9. Put It All Together   65

10. Implement Your Plans   70

11. Eighteen Months from Now   82

12. How Can I Know If I Need a Coach?   84

Endnotes   89

About the Author   93

Introduction

There is great satisfaction in knowing we are being used by God, making a difference and seeing the fruit of our efforts. A sense of purpose gives us energy and makes us look forward to getting up and going every morning.

As we think about a life of purpose, what can easily come to mind is those we hear about or know that God has used for great impact. They stand out, and we can envy them a little while recognizing that we are not them and we don't want to be.

We might hear our pastor talk about how God can use us by sharing the gospel, praying for others, serving, or going on a mission trip. Of course, if we occasionally do any or all these things, it will bring us a sense of purpose and fulfillment. But even if we did them, a fulfilling life encompasses more than these things.

As a follower of Jesus, we know intuitively that our greatest satisfaction will come from knowing God is using us to have a positive influence in others' lives. Sometimes God may use us in a big way, but most often, God will use us in many small ways. This can happen while focused on other things, but to experience this with more consistency requires knowing and intentionally living out our purpose.

Purpose gives us clarity. Rick Warren says,

Without a clear purpose you have no foundation on which you base decisions, allocate your time, and use your resources. You will tend to make choices based on circumstances, pressures, and your mood at that moment. People who don't know their purpose try to do too much—and that causes stress, fatigue, and conflict.[1]

Purpose gives us direction. Rick Warren also says, "Without a clear purpose, you will keep changing directions, jobs, relationships, churches, or other externals—hoping each change will settle the confusion or fill the emptiness in your heart."[2]

I am sure you recognize many things in your life that are good, making you feel blessed. But maybe there is also a lingering sense that something is missing. Something is still not quite right. Even though you know you are blessed, if your life is not as fulfilling as you would like, I get it. I am still on the journey and still learning, but with guidance and diligence, I have experienced a dramatic change in my own sense of fulfillment and contentment.

Through coaching others as well as through my own journey, my sense of fulfillment and contentment is now a nine (out of ten) coming from a five when I started this journey many years ago. My hope is that sharing some client stories (names changed to protect privacy) and what I have learned will help you refocus and get clarity and then get going doing what you know you were called to do. I want to help you hear from God as you ask Him to show you where to focus and how to invest your resources—your time, opportunities, money, and abilities—to do what He is leading you to do.

Like you, I am a pilgrim on the journey seeking to know how God wants to use me and then striving to go do it, with the hopeful humility to realize I need God in every part of what I do.

By helping others sort out what God is leading them to do and take steps toward it, I've learned some useful things you don't generally find all in one place. So here is one more book on the topic of life purpose. If God uses it to give you some insight, I would love to know about it.

The key to living a life of purpose isn't just about how you can do more at church or pray more for others, although that is valuable and might be a part. This is more about how to live your life every day in dependence on God, with a purpose that feels both natural and fulfilling.

Chapter 1

Where Are You Now?

Do you ever look at your life and think, *I know I'm blessed . . . so why does something still feel missing?* You love Jesus, you're grateful for what God has done in your life, and yet there's this quiet ache that your everyday life should feel fuller—richer— than it does now. Maybe you're involved at church or you tried stepping into meaningful activities, hoping they would fill that emptiness. But the feeling lingers. And you wonder, sometimes in the quiet moments, *Lord . . . is there something more You want me to do?*

Perhaps you're stepping into a new season—retirement, an empty nest, or another transition that has reshaped what purpose looks like for you. What once gave you direction has changed, and now you're not sure where to aim your energy or passion. You want to make a difference. You're willing. You're available. You just don't know what "next" should be.

Or maybe you're more like I was—faithful, engaged, doing all the right things on paper—yet carrying a subtle but persistent longing for something different . . . something deeper . . . something that aligns more fully with the way God designed you.

If that resonates, you're not alone. And you're not off track. You may simply be on the edge of a new season God is inviting you into.

Because I knew my life was good and I felt blessed, the source of my emptiness was hard to pinpoint. I had reached my long-held goal of becoming a wealth advisor with the faith-driven firm I most respected, Ronald Blue & Co. (now BlueTrust). I had achieved many of the other goals I'd set for myself and was living the life I had worked toward for years. I was active in my church, leading a Bible study and serving on a couple of boards. By most measures, things were going well.

And yet, my stress level was high. I found myself getting irritated too easily. I had good days, but many nights I went to bed frustrated with how the day had unfolded. With so much going right, why wasn't I feeling the fulfillment I expected? Was I desiring the wrong things without realizing it? Were my expectations unrealistic? Something felt missing, and unfulfilled longings continued to haunt me.

Around that time, I met a new friend who happened to be a life coach. I hired him to help me uncover some of my blind spots. Through his coaching, I began to understand my strengths more clearly—what energized me and what drained me. He helped me appreciate the unique way God created me. He challenged me to stop comparing my life to others and to let go of the unrealistic persona I had been trying to maintain. He helped me look forward to starting my day connecting with God, seeking to know Him more deeply. He taught me to trust God when things didn't go as expected. His guidance brought a growing sense of contentment and a clearer picture of how I could better use my unique design in ways that would bring greater fulfillment.

A couple of years later, I met Lloyd Reeb. He was facilitating sessions in a coaching program with Kingdom Advisors that I was part of. As a Halftime coach, Lloyd is known for asking the kind of disruptive questions that make you think about things you've never considered—but immediately recognize as important.

Wrestling with Lloyd's questions made me realize that God was trying to get my attention and prepare me for a new season. With a growing uncertainty about my path ahead, I asked Lloyd to coach me through the Halftime process. That journey helped me see how God had equipped me and how He was calling me to leave my dream job as a wealth advisor to become a Halftime coach and start a private charitable foundation.

By the time I finished my coaching with Lloyd, I had a much clearer sense of purpose. I began using my unique design to serve in roles that fit my sweet spot. I re-ordered my life priorities, which helped me focus on my purpose in every key area and pursue God-directed outcomes. I gained clarity about how to help the most important people in my life thrive—and I began doing that with intentionality.

I had to learn to let go of my own ideas about what the "best life" looked like. The more I let God set the direction, reveal the path, and guide the pace, the more my sense of purpose grew—and the more He was able to use me. Today, I experience a level of contentment, fulfillment, and peace I didn't know was possible. The emptiness, the stress, and the sense that something was missing—once a frequent companion—are now rare.

Being able to articulate what I was feeling was a key part of beginning the journey to get where I am today. We must know where we are before we can get to where we want to be. I heard versions of the below statements expressed by those I have coached when we were getting started. Do any of these resonate with you?

- A significant season of life has come to an end, and I am not sure what I want to do in this emerging new season.

- I am trying to find ways to be more intentional in how I reflect Jesus in my business/work, or in my family.

- I have been very successful in my career, but it no longer brings the satisfaction it once did.

- I have been successful, but some important relationships have not received appropriate attention, and I am not sure how to reengage with them.

- I no longer enjoy my work (or business) like I once did, but this is who I am. I don't know who I would be if I retired (or sold my business).

- I am experiencing burnout and realize I need a reset but not sure how I want to reposition myself going forward.

- I am good at what I do and compensated well, but I want to have more meaningful impact in my work.

- I don't feel like Jesus is working through me, but I am not sure what to do so God can use me more effectively.

- I have been serving God, but I also feel spiritually dry.

- It feels like I am doing all the right things, but I don't know why I am not seeing the results.

- I have been trying to transition into a new purpose-driven life but seem to be stuck and don't know how to get going.

🔑 KEY EXERCISE

Looking through the above statements, can you state in your own words where you are now?

Next, we will look back to how you got to where you are today.

Chapter 2

What Got You Here?

As we move through life, not only does our perspective change, but also our longings. Before embracing our lives ahead, it's helpful to take a moment and think about the past. Our motivations may be different, but often there are clues and patterns we can recognize that help us think about what is possible and craft a good plan for what we will do next.

We look back at key points in our lives and feel some satisfaction that they were good times—warm memories of time with family, when we were at our best, milestones of personal accomplishments. We remember times when we had some part in making a significant impact, either in the life of someone important to us or through our part in an endeavor. Times when we know without a doubt God moved in a miraculous way, reminding us that He is always there.

Perhaps among the most valuable are when we have seen those important to us thrive in their own lives. It's helpful to remember people who had a huge positive impact in our lives, and why they did. There may be some painful times that shaped who we are in a good way.

One way to jog your memory is to think about your life in decades, before twenty then each decade until now. Looking back at those key points, take a sheet of paper and write down what comes to mind. Ask God to help you recall what happened that you want in your description of what has made your life good. The more vivid the detail, the more value will come from the exercise.

When I did this, I was amazed at what I had forgotten—moments that were not always life-changing but left a huge impression. I gained a sense of perspective that helped see how what happened in the past could shape what might be coming. This also helped me look with great anticipation to what was ahead.

At the same time, you may look back and feel some regret about how things turned out, especially with some of the people that are important to you. Of course you can't change the past, but you can acknowledge it and ask God to work through you to change the future. With God's guidance, commit to build better relationships. That motivation may be a key component of what you want to focus on in this current or emerging season of life.

🔑 KEY EXERCISE

Using the prompts above, write down your thoughts about key parts of your life. Consider listing them at first, then go back and attempt to describe in more detail some of the most meaningful parts.

Chapter 3

What If Everything Turned Out As You Hoped?

As we look ahead or enter a new season of our lives, we have hopes and desires, but the uncertainty of what every day will be like leaves questions about whether life will be as good as we hoped. We may make plans to do certain things, and they happen, but then everyday life sets in, and we know we don't want to just live for the next scheduled special trip or event.

You have experienced good times before—when you felt engaged and were making a difference, when your important relationships were strong and mutually edifying, when God was working through you to bring about something significant. Take a moment to stop and think. If everything turned out exactly as you hoped in this season of life (or a new season you are about to enter), what would that look like? What would be the elements that make your life fulfilling?

This is not a quest to create a perfect life. If God is using you to have impact and make a difference, life will be fulfilling, but at times it will be hard. Things will happen that don't make sense or seem right. Daily renewing your trust in God helps bring peace when you are struggling. Isaiah 26:3–4 says, "You will keep in perfect peace all who trust in you, all whose thoughts are fixed on you! Trust in the Lord always, for the Lord God is the eternal Rock" (NLT).

Seeking to know what it means to have a fulfilling life is an opportunity to spend some time with God, seeking His will for you. Proverbs 3:5–6 is a good reminder of how God wants to guide us: "Trust in the Lord with all your heart and lean not on your own understanding; in all your ways submit to him, and he will make your paths straight" (NIV).

🔑 KEY EXERCISE

Ask God to reveal what He wants you to know about your life ahead, what He wants you to pursue and focus on. Take a sheet of paper and write down what comes to mind. If some of these things are already going well and you want it to continue, include them on the list. Ignore for the moment how you will make it happen and think of what could be if everything turned out as you hoped.

Here are some prompts to get you thinking:

- *Who would be a regular part of your life? What would you do together?*

- *What would you accomplish or focus on?*

- *What desired outcomes, in your life or those important to you, would you like to see?*

- *Where would you engage and serve in some manner?*

- *Where would you have the most meaningful impact?*

- *How would you help those important to you thrive?*

- *How would God use you in others' lives?*

- *What do you want more of in your life? Less of?*

- *If you expect to continue working, what is the joy you experience from what you do?*

- *What hobbies would you enjoy?*

- *What groups would you stay with or join?*

- *What would every day be like? Every week?*

- *What would your spiritual life be like?*

- *What would your relationship with Jesus be like?*

- *What would be different from today?*

- *What else comes to mind? What is God stirring, even if the details feel a little fuzzy?*

Thinking about the above, embedded in what you write down will be the elements of a life that brings deep joy and meaning. How does God show up in each one?

How close do you feel to this right now? Will the path you are currently on get you there? What would need to change for you to get there?

When our options diminish with age and life circumstances

I want to add a special note for those continuing to reach new milestone birthdays. A coaching client who just turned eighty said, "God allows us to reach a certain age for a reason, and we've got to continually be aware of that reason." As we get older, it can become more challenging to identify that reason God still has us here, but we cannot forget that God always has a purpose, and we are not finished until He calls us home.

Over my life, I have had many friends in their 70s, 80s and 90s that help me gain a greater perspective on life. I enjoy being with them and hearing their stories, yet they don't live in the past. They have hopes, ambitions and a sense of purpose, and they look forward to getting up every day.

Our culture doesn't expect you to be engaged as you get older but to relax and enjoy life. And they add, "You've paid your dues. Let the younger ones take on the responsibility." But you think differently. You know you're not done.

It's nice to be able to slow the pace down, spend more time with those you love, enjoy the blessings of life that can too easily be taken for granted, and be available when someone needs you. But that isn't enough. You have the motivation, the capacity, and the energy to do more than you are doing.

Bob Buford wrote a book called *Finishing Well*. In the foreword to the book, Ken Blanchard writes that Bob "talked to 120 exceptional people—folks he called 'code breakers'"[3] A common theme Bob found was that this group didn't just let things happen. Peter Drucker, his mentor and famous father of modern management, said these folks think ahead and are introspective.[4] Using a common business term, they found ways to pivot as circumstances changed by engaging in outside the box thinking. Some accomplished later in life what they realized was even more significant than the successful careers they left behind.

Looking at your life as it is today, what makes you want to wake up every morning and engage in something that brings deep joy and meaning? What is a good day like? Who do you want to be with? What do you like to be doing? How will God use you in others' lives? When do you feel most at peace? When do you feel joy?

Now that you have the time to do it, how is your daily quiet time with God? Is it providing peace, joy, guidance, confidence? If so, how? What's missing in your daily quiet time with God? What changes might yield greater peace, joy, and confidence?

My hope is that I can stir some ideas for you to consider and pursue. With God's guidance, what kind of life can you build?

Will others see your life and say, "_____ is finishing well"?

Chapter 4

Experience a Fulfilling Life of Purpose

A fulfilling life—one rich in joy, meaning, and purpose—relies on a few essential ingredients. Neglect any of them, and the journey becomes harder and less rewarding. Include them all, and you'll be ready to seize new opportunities and walk the road with those who matter most.

Here are the essentials for living a purposeful, impactful life.

Our platforms are the places where we're known and where we have influence or impact. Each of us has more than one platform, and on every platform we play a role. That role may not always come with a title, but it defines how we show up, interact, and make a difference. We'll explore your platforms and the unique role you have on each one.

Our purpose reflects what stirs our hearts—our drive to solve a problem, make something better, or serve, teach, or mentor others. We'll explore what God has uniquely called you to do, how that calling meets real needs, and the impact it can leave behind. We'll also look at what you're passionate about and what outcome you desire as you live out your purpose.

Our valuable relationships are the people who matter most. They give our lives depth and meaning. We'll take time to look at your relationships and identify who you most want to invest in and prioritize.

Our unique design includes our experiences, our talents, our strengths and abilities, our spiritual gifts, our core values, our financial resources, our personality. We will explore how you are uniquely designed and equipped to live out the purpose God has for you.

Living a fulfilling life with purpose begins with seeking God's guidance to understand how He wants to use us—and combining that with some intentional, strategic planning. The planning isn't complicated, but it is essential. It helps us bring everything together to create the kind of journey we long for: a purposeful, fulfilling life that is being used by God.

One of the challenges, however, is that this isn't a neat or predictable process. Life is messy. We'll face delays, setbacks, and disappointments that force us to adjust our expectations and approaches along the way. As our journey unfolds, we must keep seeking God's will—trusting that He'll reveal new insights, opportunities, and sometimes even closed doors.

The key is to stay adaptable and resilient. As Lloyd Reeb says, "If we infuse intentionality but insist on the outcomes, we become miserable. If we infuse intentionality and remain open and flexible, looking for opportunities that come our way, then it blossoms into something that brings joy and enables us to produce a compounding impact."[5]

It's good to have desired outcomes—they give us direction and purpose—but we must commit to being intentional without trying to control the process or the results.

In the following chapters, we'll look deeper at the essential elements that make up a fulfilling, purpose-driven life.

Chapter 5

Be Intentional with Your Platforms

A platform is a place where you are known. You have more than one platform and they are not necessarily a physical place. Your presence on a platform matters. It is on your platforms that God will work through you living out the purpose He has for you. When you are clear on your purpose and role on each platform, you can serve there and have impact with more intentionality.

Jesus left Nazareth and relocated to Capernaum to begin His earthly ministry (see Matt. 4:13). This location became one of His key platforms for His ministry. As Jim Denison points out, this wasn't a random choice of location. Capernaum sat on the northern shore of the Sea of Galilee and served as a hub of both political and commercial activity in the region. As a thriving fishing port that drew both Jewish and Gentile populations, it functioned as one of the most influential centers in all of Galilee. By establishing His ministry headquarters in this strategic, cosmopolitan town rather than in a quieter, more isolated community, Jesus positioned Himself to reach the widest possible audience with His message. It was, according to Jim Denison, the "New York City of Galilee—a place of strategic influence."[6]

Identify Your Platforms

To identify your platforms, start with looking at where you already have influence, are engaged in some manner, or have some part in getting things done. What could this include? Your workplace/business, your family, your household, your church, a group where you regularly interact? Is there any other place where you have some sort of role or a consistent and known presence? Although your degree of influence and impact may vary, all of these are your platforms. Ask family members to help you make a list of your platforms.

In some cases, you may prefer the word community to the word platform. In every community of which you are a part, you are known and have some sort of influence. Your influence may be significant, or it may be minimal. Whether platform or community is the way you see it, where are you known and are present?

On each of your platforms, you will also have a role. It may or may not be a formal role with a title, but your role indicates the context of how you interact on each platform (or within each community).

As an example, here are my current platforms and my role on each one:

Platform	Role
God's kingdom	Follower of Jesus
My household	Husband, partner, and provider
My extended family	Father, father-in-law, grandfather
Halftime[7]	Executive coach and facilitator
Ferry Charitable Foundation	President and chairman of the board
Faith-Driven Entrepreneur Group	Facilitator
Our church	Active member, giver, and volunteer leader
Sunday morning Bible study	Class member
Guys' group in our community	Friend and regular attender
Personal board of directors	Organizer, mutual advisor, sounding board, accountability partner, friend
My siblings	Brother, brother-in-law, first born
Wife's siblings	Brother-in-law
Las Colinas community	Community resident and volunteer leader
Kingdom Advisors study group	Regular attendee

We often think of a *platform* as a place outside our home—somewhere we're active and have a role to play. But viewing our household and family as one of our platforms can feel uncomfortable, as if it's self-serving or self-focused.

The truth is, God has placed each of us in our families for a purpose. Just like other platforms where we have influence, our home is a place where He wants to work through us. When we're intentional, we can actively love and serve our family, allowing God's love to flow through us in meaningful ways.

If we're not intentional, though, we can easily miss those opportunities to bless the people closest to us. Our purpose within our household isn't about focusing on ourselves—it's about being others-focused, which often doesn't come naturally.

🔑 KEY EXERCISE

Make a list of your platforms. Remember that a platform can be both a physical place (e.g., your household, where you work, your church), and a distinct group where you have influence, are engaged in some manner, or you have some part in getting things done. What is your role on each of the platforms you have named?

Are you where God wants you to be?

Your various platforms are where you are living your life. Obviously, some of your platforms will never change and always be part of your life (e.g., parent, child, sibling, etc.), while other platforms you chose to be on.

Remember earlier it was mentioned that Jesus left Nazareth and relocated to Capernaum to begin His earthly ministry.

Sometimes God calls us to leave a platform and go to a new one. Or instead, God may have us remain on a platform where we are already known and have influence but focus on a different purpose. Looking at your platforms, do you sense God leading you to change your focus on any of them? Or should you consider leaving one or more of your "chosen" platforms, because your impact has diminished or the purpose for being there has changed?

God called Elizabeth and me to leave behind well-established platforms based where we lived in South Florida for twenty seven years and where our kids grew up and relocate to Colorado, 2,100 miles away. How did we know God wanted us to move? Both Elizabeth and I could see our roles on several of our South Florida based platforms coming to an end for different reasons. Our kids had moved away and made it clear they had no intentions of returning to South Florida to live. God also instilled in us both a desire to live in the mountains of Colorado and experience the Colorado lifestyle.

At first it wasn't completely clear why God was leading us to Colorado. We made several trips, determined where God wanted us to live, and got to know people there. We bought a second home, and God began to show us the platforms He wanted us both to explore. We knew there still was risk that such a drastic move might not turn out as we expected, but everything seemed to indicate it was time to be there full time.

We stepped out in obedience, sold our home in South Florida and moved. Soon after, we learned that for Elizabeth the timing was for the ministry purpose God had for her, discipling young moms in a ministry based at our church. After a couple of years of serving, she was asked to take on a leadership role. God worked through her to have an incredible impact.

After we made the move, God guided me to lead a ministry at our church helping others discover and pursue God's purpose for their lives. We helped over a hundred people explore God's purpose. Two couples were able to discern God's call to the mission field full time, and another discerned God called him to leave an executive position in the business world and become a full-time pastor.

Several years later, Elizabeth's ministry leadership role had come to an end, as well as my role leading the church ministry. At about the same time God revealed a new purpose for us that necessitated making another move. We felt the call to live near our daughter, son-in-law, and grandchildren. Confirming this was from God, we relocated again to Central Florida.

Relocating over halfway across the United States is a big change. We took it one step at a time, testing whether we heard God correctly before taking the next step. As we kept moving forward with the next step, we found ways to limit the risk that this wouldn't work out as we expected. But at some point, we had to make the bigger commitments, trusting that we heard God's purpose for what He was leading us to do.

If God is leading you to leave one platform and go to another, it will most likely be less disruptive than moving 2,100 miles. It may be as simple as starting a new Bible study and leaving another study behind. Or resigning from a role in an organization to serve elsewhere. Or deciding to join a new group of people to build relationships so God can use you there. Change always brings some uncertainty, which brings risk that it may not work out. Taking baby steps can help gain clarity, and we adjust our plans as we gain new information.

There is comfort in the familiar, and it is usually easier to stay than go to something new. Doubt about whether a change is really what God wants us to do can also make us hesitate and stay where we are, rather than seek God's guidance about our purpose. Again, Proverbs 3:5–6 comes to mind as a reminder to ask for God's guidance, "Trust in the Lord with all your heart and lean not on your own understanding; in all your ways submit to Him, and He will make your paths straight" (NIV).

If God is prompting you to make a change in one or more of your platforms, are you open to His leading? Are you willing to consider a new purpose for one or more of your platforms? Are you willing to try out a new platform to see if that is where God is leading you to engage for impact? A new platform will likely be a place where you already have some connections, which provides the opportunity to learn more about it before making a commitment.

We have all had the experience of taking on a role with great anticipation, only later to discover it was nothing like what we expected, and we feel stuck. The more you know, the greater the confidence that joining a new platform is what God is calling you to do. If someone is pressuring you to commit quickly on a new platform, pray for discernment and ask if you can engage on a trial basis for a few weeks or months before you say yes.

How can God work more effectively through you on your various platforms?

As mentioned earlier, one of Elizabeth's platforms was a ministry in Colorado discipling young moms. I saw her commitment and consistency, and this gave her influence. It was on this platform that God called Elizabeth to become a leader, increasing her impact and influence.

Often, the place where God is calling you to make the greatest impact isn't somewhere new—it's one of your current platforms, right where He's already placed you. What is your role? It may or may not be a formal role with a title, but your role indicates the context of how you interact on each platform. Ask God to help you discern the value of your involvement in your current platforms and how you interact there. Is God leading you to take on a different role (more engaged or less engaged)? For as long as you remain on a platform, pray for His guidance as to how you can maximize your impact.

As a life and leadership coach, I have worked with many business owners that had established a successful business but were feeling the prompting for a change. They wrestled with whether they should sell their business and move on or remain in the business as one of their platforms and take on a different role.

Ed started and built a highly successful business in trucking and logistics. He decided to hire a CEO and executive team and remain in his role as owner but not leader of the business. He engages in setting strategic direction for the business and serving as an advisor to his leadership team, but he has changed his primary focus to starting and funding ministries where he and his wife have a passion to serve unmet needs among some of the most neglected people groups.

Steve was CEO of a multi-billion dollar construction company. He stepped down as CEO and his son took on that role, leading the company into more success. Then Steve stepped down as chairman of the board and moved off the board. He is still a co-owner and now focuses on being an informal connector for the business, an encourager to the thousands of employees they have, and an engaged leader in local charitable endeavors.

🔑 KEY EXERCISE

Take some time to evaluate your current platforms and your role on each one. What is God showing you? What platforms will you continue? What platforms should you leave behind? What platforms are you considering joining or starting? Which of your roles on each platform will you continue doing, and which roles might you want to change?

Chapter 6

Get Clear About Your Purpose

Trying to discern our life purpose can feel like a daunting task. When we know people who have a clear life purpose and we see them living it out, it can be discouraging when we don't have clarity of our own life purpose.

God gives some people a clear life purpose, such as Billy Graham. The apostle Paul was a Pharisee hunting down followers of Jesus; then God called him to become a great leader in the early church. Peter was a fisherman called to the Jews as his mission field. James, Jesus's half-brother, became the pastor of the first church in Christian history. Paul, Peter, and James entered their primary life purpose in midlife, then lived the rest of their lives carrying out God's unique purpose for them.[8]

Like the examples above, for many years I operated under the belief that I should know my life purpose, then go live that out. For a few people I know they have this level of clarity and focus. But for me and most of those I have coached, it isn't this simple.

God gives most of us purpose for a season. A "season" can vary in length of time from a few months to many years. And in each season we may have more than one purpose, tied to more than one of our roles on more than one of our platforms. I didn't have to figure out my entire life purpose. Instead, I could focus on what God had for me in my current season of life, which made it much easier to discern how He wanted to use me.

Does God call us to where He wants to use us?

A term that can be misunderstood and misapplied is the term *calling*, but I think it fits with how God wants us to live out our purpose. We tend to view calling in the church as only applying to those that are called to be pastors or priests or missionaries. The rest of us go get jobs or start businesses so we can make enough money to live and give to the church. Our work is viewed as nothing more than a way to make a living, and our real purpose doesn't come from our work. Of course, we want to celebrate all of those that answer God's call to become pastors or missionaries, but I believe limiting it to this only is a fundamental misunderstanding of the word calling. Based on what the Bible is saying, I believe God calls every follower of Jesus to something, and that calling will be connected to a unique purpose God has for each of us, reflecting how God wants to use us.

If we view our work for which we are being paid as our calling, God can use us on that platform if we invite Him to do so. I know with much conviction that God called me to and prepared me for the work I engaged in, and this was in two sequential roles with two different purposes in two different seasons of life. And before I took advantage of these two work opportunities, I prayed for clarity that this was what God was calling me to do.

On the website Faith Driven Entrepreneur[9] we see many examples of clear purpose on the platform of business. There is a story about Pete Ochs who owns Seat King. One of his challenges was finding good employees, so he went into Hutchinson Correctional Facility to hire inmates. Pete treats each employee within the prison with dignity and respect and builds a deep relationship with them, and then he says "we let the Lord figure out how to open those doors of spiritual capital."[10] As one employee said, Pete "brought hope in a dark place."[11]

Louie, one of Pete's employees, was up for parole. Pete was out of the country and flew back to speak for Louie at his parole hearing. Louie got out of prison and learned to be a tattoo artist. He wanted to open his own tattoo studio, and Pete helped Louie figure out a business plan to launch his business.

Pete is clear about his purpose on the platform of his business. He says, "In business, we become hardened to the bottom line. . . . Business is really about people. We should be in business to really transform society. When we started to really love those guys as we loved ourselves, we saw transformation happen. It really gave me a whole new vision for what I could to as a businessperson."[12]

In addition to being called to a job or a business, we are also called to serve in roles that are not a job. First Corinthians 7:17 says, "Each of you should continue to live in whatever situation the Lord has placed you, and remain as you were when God first called you" (NLT). A friend recently reminded me that if I have kids, I have been called by God to be a father for my children. I have been called as a husband to my wife. I have other callings as well, and although some will change, callings from God don't stop just because I have retired from full-time work for which I was compensated. God will continue to have callings for each of us until we leave this world, but of course some of our callings can change when we grow older.

God doesn't need us, but He calls us to join Him and be co-laborers with Him, making a difference where we live and interact with others. It's important that we seek God's guidance for our calling, because He is the one that prepared us for what He has for us to do. Ephesians 2:10 says, "For we are God's masterpiece. He has created us anew in Christ Jesus, so we can do the good things He planned for us long ago" (NLT). If we submit to His guidance, God will take the combination of our talents, strengths, passions, preparation, experience, personality, and motivation, pointing all that toward something where He can work through us most effectively. It may only be for a season of a few weeks to a few years, but our calling is how God wants to work through us.

One of the easiest places to seek purpose is through our church. In addition to supporting our church financially, God also calls us to serve. And because we hear a regular reminder of people needed for different things in the church, out of a feeling of guilt we may volunteer, even if we are not sure God wants us to step up. I have had many different roles at my church. Some were good and others didn't work out so well. Since there always seem to be multiple serving opportunities, now I ask God to guide me to where He is calling me to serve.

We must also be careful not to wait for the perfect fitting role. Elizabeth's call to serve in a leadership role in the ministry to young moms came through our church. She didn't feel prepared and struggled with whether she should say yes. But following her sense of the Holy Spirit to accept the call, she took the leap and God used her to have great impact.

We know God is sovereign over the marketplace, over the workplace, over our home and over our relationships, but He will not force us to submit all we do to His direction. We can easily get into the habit of functioning in those arenas out of our own strengths and intuition, seeking His help only when we get in trouble. Wherever we experience life, God calls us as His followers to make a difference, but not as an afterthought. Not only do I ask God to reveal my purpose on each platform, but I also frequently pray that God will reveal His purpose in my daily interactions in all aspects of my life, making me aware of the opportunities and preparing me to be used.

God wants to work through all of us if we invite Him to do so and are willing to be teachable and obedient. How much more could God use us if we seek His guidance about where and how we do what He is calling us to do in every sphere of our life, and on every platform where He has us?

How can God show me what He is leading me to do?

When you think about it, you realize that on many of your platforms you are already carrying out one of your purposes. As you look at each one, is a change needed to be more aligned with God's purpose on that platform?

Are you clear about your purpose on each of your platforms, or is it too broad or too vague? For example, if you are a father and grandfather, your purpose would be to love your children and grandchildren. That sounds right but is somewhat broad, and there are many ways you can do that. To make it clearer, what is it you really want for them? What are your desired outcomes for them? What could make the greatest difference? How might God use you in bringing that about?

God can choose to make His purpose known in many ways, because He is God. Spending time daily in the Bible is important because God's Word is a prime source for His guidance. If we are seeking to follow God's leading and not our own whims, the motivation to do something is also a good indicator. Before moving forward, I ask God to confirm my desires and motivations with a sense of peace before proceeding.

Terry Looper in his book *Sacred Pace* shares how he waits on God to direct his actions. He begins each day prayerfully asking God, "What's next? What is Your plan for me?" Then he reads from his Bible and a devotion. He adds, "If I submitted myself to the Lord's wisdom, He would simultaneously direct my steps and ensure that my heart's desires echoed my heavenly Father's desires for me. That was the burst of faith I needed to rest in the Lord until He advised my next move."[13]

In some cases, especially for those people most important to you in a difficult situation, your purpose is to serve them in their time of need. It could be a family member suffering from a major illness or injury. Out of love and caring about their welfare, you can't imagine abandoning them, although it can sometimes be hard and exhausting.

There are always many possibilities to engage, but only a few that are a good fit. How can you know what is best for you? Another key to God's purpose is something you never tire of working on, you never tire of talking about. God gives each of us a passion—an emotional stirring—for what He wants us to focus on. Our zeal for solving a problem, making something better, or serving others keeps us motivated when it gets hard to do. What stirs you emotionally? What makes you stop and pay attention? What do family members and close friends comment that you are always talking about? What makes you sad, mad, or glad when you hear about it? Have you felt that same emotion more than once about what is stirring you? If so, what desired outcomes are you seeing that makes you want to engage and keep going? The lingering emotion that keeps getting stirred can be a clue to what God is calling you to focus on.

When seeking clarity about your purpose, beware of others trying to recruit you to do something. When they are so passionate about it, with good intentions and sincerity they believe you should also be doing what God has called them to do. In the body of Christ God gives each of us different gifts (see Rom. 12:4-6 and 1 Cor. 12:4-11). God calls each of us to different purposes and He equips us for the purpose He has for us. As Ephesians 2:10 reminds us, "For we are his workmanship, created in Christ Jesus for good works, which God prepared beforehand, that we should walk in them" (ESV). If you are personally interested in what someone is recruiting you to do, explore it further. But instead, your role may be to encourage them in what they feel called to do.

Whether we feel called or not, during times of a crisis or emergency we should be willing to respond to a need. The parable of the good Samaritan reminds us that in these special situations it's "All hands on deck!" regardless of skill or motivation. Proverbs 2:1-6 reminds us to seek clarity from God before taking on a role that may require a longer commitment. If we're not wired and equipped for a role and don't feel called, the risk of burnout and resentment is higher if serving there for a longer period.

🔑 KEY EXERCISE

God has given you a passion for what He is calling you to focus on. Your zeal for solving a problem, making something better, or serving others keeps you motivated when it gets hard to do. Pay attention to what stirs you emotionally. What makes you stop and pay attention? What do family members and close friends comment that you are always talking about? What makes you sad, mad, or glad when you hear about it? Have you felt that same emotion more than once about what is stirring you? Write out what is coming to mind. What is a desired outcome you would like to see from pursuing this?

Will God give us more than one primary purpose?

Just as we have more than one platform, God will likely have more than one purpose for us—perhaps a different purpose on each platform. We may have a primary purpose and other secondary purposes. Each purpose is important, but our primary purpose is where God is calling us to focus most of our energy, our time, our talent, and perhaps our treasure.

When I say primary purpose, the context is usually a key role for us outside of our roles related to our family. When we're working, it is easier to identify that as our primary purpose. If we're volunteering outside our home, but not working for pay, the best way to clarify whether it is a primary purpose would be if it will require a significant ongoing commitment of our time and energy.

We may not have what we would consider a primary purpose, and instead several purposes that all seem equally as valuable. As we consider our various platforms and seek God's guidance as to what He wants us to focus on there, we will begin to see God's purpose for us on each platform.

I had to learn how to identify God's purpose for me on each of my platforms. Two of my platforms—Halftime and the charitable foundation—are my primary purpose, meaning this is where I put most of my time and energy. On the Halftime[14] platform, in my role as a life and leadership coach, I get to live out my purpose of helping others know and live out God's purpose for their lives. I never get tired of doing it. On the charitable foundation platform, I get to live out my purpose of being used by God to make others' lives better, spreading the love of Jesus by providing support for organizations called to serve a purpose. Another way I might describe my foundation role is an informed donor or silent partner. I never get tired of doing it. I can also define my purpose on every other platform where I am engaged, but they don't require as much of my time and energy.

One key indicator that God has revealed to you your purpose(s) is when you never tire of working on it, you never tire of talking about it. William Barclay tells us: "A man will never become outstandingly good at anything unless that thing is his ruling passion. There must be something of which he can say, 'For me to live is this.' What is your "ruling passion"?[15]

🔑 KEY EXERCISE

Look at all your platforms and identify your purpose for each.

Here are some questions to get you thinking:

- *Is your purpose clear? If not, what can you do to get more clarity?*

- *Would writing out your desired outcome help clarify your purpose there?*

- *As you think about your purpose on some of your platforms, is that an indicator it may be time to leave that platform? Or do you believe God still wants you on that platform and you need more clarity about His purpose for you there?*

- *Is God revealing a purpose for you that is not yet getting carried out on any of your current platforms? Does that purpose need to be connected to one or more existing platforms, or does this mean you need to join or start another platform to live out this purpose?*

Chapter 7

Make the Important People in Your Life a Priority

One of the ways God wants to use us on our journey is most likely connected to the people in our lives. As we go through our day, we encounter many people. A good friend of mine loves to talk with everyone he sees. He brings a little of God's love to their day, and he gets energized from their conversation.

God uses us in relationships, and those relationships give our lives meaning. But if we want a deeper relationship than casual conversation, we must recognize our capacity constraints and decide who to focus on.

Here is an example of how focusing on someone important helps us discern our purpose. A good friend sold his oil and gas company and retired from the business. He was approached by his two boys to help them launch an oil and gas company, to learn from their father what made him so successful in oil and gas. He is delighted to have the opportunity to mentor them. While he didn't have the desire to get back into it, he started a business with his two sons. What would you be willing to do that could build a strong relationship with your children, and allow them to see how God works through you in everyday life?

Who are the people God is calling you to prioritize in your life?

God's purpose for your platforms is most likely tied to focusing on the people on each platform. Who all does that include? Establishing a priority ranking for all the people in your life also reflects the importance of each platform.

As an example, God led me to the following ranking of the people in my life. Each of these persons(s) are on one of my platforms listed previously:

- Elizabeth (my spouse)

- Our children and their spouses, and our grandchildren

- My colleagues in Halftime and those I coach in Halftime

- My colleagues in the foundation I lead, and the leaders of the organizations we partner with in the foundation

- My fellow members of my personal board of directors

- A few close friends that I want to support and enjoy life with

- My siblings and their spouses

- Elizabeth's siblings and their spouses

- People in the groups I facilitate, such as Faith Driven Entrepreneurs

- Our Sunday morning Bible study group

- Guys group in our community

- Las Colinas neighbors

All the above are important or I wouldn't include them. You may decide to approach setting priorities differently, but establishing rankings with groups of people will help you make those difficult choices when you can't do all you want to do or are being asked to do.

How can you make those important to you a priority?

One of God's purposes for you is probably connected to what you want to do for the most important people in your life. But what does that really look like?

Start by thinking about how you can truly serve them. Sure, being supportive and present matters—that's the foundation. But I think it also means helping them thrive and flourish.

For me, that's looked like taking a real interest in who they are—what drives them, what excites them, and what challenges they're facing. I've also had to let go of the need to impress them and just be open about my own struggles. When I started doing that, I noticed something change. The relationships got deeper, more honest, and more life-giving—for them and for me.

I coached a guy that was brilliant at sharing God in creative ways with his young grandchildren. Rick lived down the street from his two kids and their families, and he got to spend a lot of time with his grandchildren. He walked them to school and went to meet them and walk them home. When together he would point out things in nature and marvel at how God created the world for us to enjoy. Imagine the impact on a young child's life by helping him/her to see the glory of God all around them.

If some of the important people in your life don't yet have a relationship with Jesus, one of God's purposes for you may be to help point them toward Him. Sometimes that happens through sharing the gospel directly—but as you probably know, they might not always be ready to hear it.

You can (and should) pray for their salvation, but God can also use your life and your words to spark their curiosity about Him. Share, when it feels right, how your faith has helped you through challenges or brought you peace and joy. Be open about your own struggles and how Jesus has walked with you through them.

You can also gently draw attention to God's presence in everyday moments—the beauty of a sunset, the wonder of nature, or the kindness of others. When they face something hard, offer to pray for them or even with them.

And when that moment comes when they're ready—when they ask about having a personal relationship with Jesus—trust the Holy Spirit to guide your words and let God work through you.

For the most important people in my life, I've also learned that God calls me to treat them as equals and show genuine respect—even if some happen to report to me in another role. The same goes for my adult children. They're no longer my responsibility to parent, and that means releasing my expectations of what I think they should do or how they should live.

God's been teaching me to resist the urge to offer unsolicited advice, even when I believe it's right or helpful. Instead, He reminds me to trust that He's at work in their lives just as He is in mine. And honestly, I've realized I don't always welcome that kind of advice either. Learning to step back, listen, and let God lead has brought more peace—and healthier relationships.

So how can we be proactive and help those important to us thrive with these self-imposed constraints? First, because it's somewhat obvious, by regularly praying for them. In addition, by seeking the opportunity to be with them with no agenda. By looking for ways to sincerely affirm them. By looking for appropriate moments to share my own stories of how God has and is working in my life, and the impact that is having. By showing interest in them and what they are doing by asking about their life and what they are experiencing, while remembering to not pepper them with so many questions that it becomes annoying.

I frequently forget how God wants to use me in little ways throughout my day. God may be prompting me to say something simple or do something that seems insignificant, and if I'm not aware, I may overlook it. So many times it's in the seemingly small things where God uses us, and I must remember that so I don't miss God's promptings.

Making other people a priority also requires remaining flexible. When they want time with me, I try to change my schedule and find a way to do it because they are a priority.

Flexibility also means being available to serve someone God brings into my life that is not a priority or not on my radar. Being very intentional by nature, I can be too focused and miss what God wants to bring to my attention. When God is nudging me to do something for someone, I must be ready to let go of my agenda and respond.

My biggest challenge regarding the most important people in my life is realizing I cannot control outcomes. I make plans to talk about something important and then the conversation doesn't go as I expected. They may not relate to what I am saying or don't want to talk about it. I had to learn how to trust God and what He is doing in their lives, letting God use me the way He wants to use me and when. As mentioned earlier, being adaptable while maintaining resilience will help us enjoy the journey. Lloyd Reeb says, "If we infuse intentionality but insist on the outcomes, we become miserable. If we infuse intentionality and we are open and flexible, looking for opportunities that come our way, then it blossoms into something that brings joy and enables us to produce a compounding impact."[16]

With those most important to me, I don't know when a breakthrough may occur or a desired milestone will be reached. When it does, I quietly celebrate the glimpses of God working in the lives of those I love, journaling what occurred. If appropriate, I tell them I see God working and that brings me joy.

🔑 KEY EXERCISE

Who are all the different groups of people in your life? What platform is each on? How would you rank them in order of priority? (If helpful, go back to my ranking of the people in my life as an example.) For the most important people, how will you make them a priority? Who do you want to love extravagantly? Thinking back to your life purposes, how does that connect to the people in your life that are most important to you?

How can I help my spouse thrive?

Marriage is a God-ordained partnership with an exceptionable level of commitment to each other. We can demonstrate love for our spouse by serving and supporting them and putting their needs ahead of our own. But the more we share with our spouse what our heart wants and needs, the deeper and more fulfilling the relationship.

Real heart-to-heart conversation happens when the person we're sharing with truly wants to understand and is willing to listen without judging or immediately trying to fix things. I strive to encourage that with Elizabeth by being a good listener, not a good fixer.

If we haven't regularly talked with someone else about our needs, wants, and desires—especially our spouse—this could be a little challenging. If previous conversations didn't go well, we may hesitate to be open. And if we are open with someone but the other person is not doing the same, we will start to hold back. Mutually agree to be vulnerable, and watch your relationship grow deeper.

One of my greatest joys is seeing Elizabeth thrive in ways I never expected. But for that to happen, I have to place her first. I put my purpose second and communicate my commitment to doing that. I had to learn how to discover what she really wants—not just what she'll settle for. I had to help her see that it's good to dream of possibilities that God brings into our lives. I had to affirm her strengths and her gifts. I had to learn to listen without trying to fix her. I had to encourage her to explore and be open to ways God was desiring to use her and live out the purpose God has for her. I blew it more than once and had to regroup and ask the Holy Spirit for guidance and try again.

For this to be successful I first shared with her what I wanted—my dreams, desires, and ambitions, and why they mattered to me. That wasn't easy for me. I also had to realize this is a journey together, exploring what God wants us to know and do. It takes time and focus to truly understand what that means. I am still learning.

My Halftime coach, Lloyd Reeb, and his wife Linda together wrote a book entitled *Halftime for Couples*.[17] The primary theme of the book is the transition at midlife from one season to the next—or, as we say at Halftime,[18] from success to significance. Whether or not someone would say they are in "halftime," there is a lot here to help couples express what they are yearning and feeling, but either don't know how to say it or don't feel like they are being heard.

Lloyd's coaching helped me see the importance of being real with each other about our desires, dreams and concerns. This seems so logical for a married couple to do, but the demands of living, of work, of children, of aging parents and their needs, can keep us focused on just getting through the day. We had to set a time when we were not hurried or distracted to talk about these things—relaxed and ready to listen to each other.

The conversation that totally changed our lives

Here is a little about our own journey as a couple. Early in our married life, Elizabeth enabled me to pursue a successful career by taking primary responsibility for things in our home, making sure all was going smoothly. She loved to cook and made sure we had good meals prepared for the family. When kids came along, she enrolled them in all the activities and served as the primary chauffer getting them to and from all they were doing. She also made sure they did their homework. Sure, I did a lot of things, but she took on the lion's share of responsibility on the home front. She had willingly placed my wants and dreams ahead of hers, freeing me to pursue mine. She seemed content with that, and presuming all was good I never initiated a conversation to talk about what she might want.

When the kids were through high school and out of the house, Elizabeth saw a lot of her identity and calling go away, but I was able to keep going with my career. With capacity to do more, she searched for places and ways to plug in, but nothing truly significant was emerging. For the first time in her life, she could do almost anything she wanted. Being focused on our family, now that she had time for other things, she had never thought much about what was next.

One day, Lloyd pointed out that much of my success in my career was possible because Elizabeth carried the greater load at home. She made it possible for me to focus on my work by taking such loving responsibility for our family and household. Now that our children were out of the house, he asked me, "Do you know Elizabeth's greatest dream?" I presumed she was already living that out, but I told him I couldn't honestly answer that question. In over thirty-five years of marriage I never questioned whether she wanted something different. Being convicted that my presumption may not be correct, I had to ask her.

Knowing this was an important question, I planned to ask one night after dinner, when the two of us were relaxed and enjoying the evening on our patio. I set it up this way. "I would like to ask you a question: What would you say is your greatest dream? I am not seeking an immediate answer. Do you want to take a week to think about it and pray about it?" Without hesitation she answered my question—and it was a complete surprise. What she said changed the course of our life. God used this to lead us to move 2,100 miles from South Florida to Colorado, where God used her in significant ways in the lives of young moms at our church.

That evening after she told me her greatest dream, I asked why she had never shared that with me. "I never told you because your business is here in South Florida. I know you love your career. If we moved to Colorado, I don't know what you would do." I knew God had planted this desire in her, and when I heard it, I felt a desire to go for it. We could see a lot of obstacles and neither of us had any idea how this might unfold. I told her I didn't know how it might happen, but I wanted to pursue what she wanted to do. For decades of our marriage she enabled me to pursue my dreams in business and in wealth management. Now it was her turn.

Pursuing Elizabeth's greatest dream changed the course of our lives, leading us on an adventure that was fun, challenging, risky, and fulfilling. We got to see God do things in ways that were clearly Him because we had no idea how some of it was going to fall into place.

What if I had never asked Elizabeth what was her greatest dream? And what if because we couldn't see how it was all going to happen, we were afraid to even start the journey? The great adventure God had for us may have never happened.

What your spouse really wants is not the same as mine and will probably not require a significant life transition. But how do we know what that is if we never bothered to ask?

🔑 KEY EXERCISE

If you have been married for a while, it's easy to presume—like I did—that you know what each other wants and likes and dislikes. You interact and do things for each other based on what you know, not realizing your spouse may have an unspoken desire for doing things different. How well do you know your spouse's needs, wants, and desires? How well do they know yours? Could your spouse desire something they never shared because you never asked? When was the last time the two of you had the opportunity to talk about the future? Talk about your hopes and dreams? Try not to let how you might do something keep you from considering it. If God is in it, He will make it happen. You may not get the immediately clarifying response I got, but starting with simpler questions may lead to new insight and direction. Can I encourage you to set aside some time to talk as a couple, when you are both relaxed and not hurried or distracted? Expect that you will need to do this more than once, and if the discussion isn't going well, don't press, and strive to be understanding. Set a time to meet again before finishing your first talk together.

Chapter 8

Harness Your Unique
Design for Your Purpose

The first disciples Jesus called were all fishermen. They weren't looking for anything different to do, but out of obedience they responded when Jesus called (Matt. 4:18–22). But why *these* four fishermen? "They were prepared," Jim Denison observes. "As fishermen, they brought skills and experiences to 'fishing for men.' Fishermen in those days must be courageous and willing to work in all kinds of weather. They must persevere, going days and nights without catching fish. They must be patient and flexible, willing to use whatever nets and methods work. And they must be humble and invisible—fish don't want to see a fisherman. All this they would need in the work to which they were called."[19]

Most of those I coach are in a time of transition. Our focus is how to discover and engage in their primary calling for their next season, outside of their roles within their family. Just like Jesus called fishermen to be His disciples because they were prepared and equipped in unique ways, one of my objectives is to help my clients gain greater clarity about their unique design. I strive to help them see that God has a purpose that gets accomplished in a key role that fits who they already are. That role will draw from their experiences, their talents, their strengths and abilities, their spiritual gifts, their core values, their personality—all reflected in their unique design. Their role will also frequently be on a platform that is very familiar to them, but their purpose has changed giving them a different focus. The skills and experiences that equip and prepare them to have impact is already there, but not yet fully deployed. With a new God-given purpose, they are eager to learn what God wants to teach them, showing them how they can take their unique design to pursue a different outcome.

When my coach first told me to take a step back and consider all dimensions of who I am, my reaction was, "I am very self-aware and know myself at this point in life. This shouldn't be hard." He suggested I engage in some assessments to identify strengths, spiritual gifts, key past experiences, core values, my passion to pursue certain things. I did the assessments he recommended, not expecting to learn anything new. I was surprised by what I discovered about myself. I learned about important unique abilities that prepared me for roles I would have never considered.

How has God prepared you for how He wants to use you?

Ephesians 2:10 says, "For we are His workmanship, created in Christ Jesus for good works, which God prepared beforehand so that we would walk in them" (NASB). God has prepared you and equipped you for the purpose He intends you to fulfill. Your experiences, your talents, your strengths and abilities, and your spiritual gifts are all part of your unique design. It will be most valuable to assess all the elements of your unique design, discovering things about yourself you never realized, especially in combination with each other.

One of the most beautiful things to see is when God works in someone and uses them to accomplish incredible impact. Knowing it's God that produces the fruit in us, we can fall into the trap of believing that for God to use us, it must be in an area of our weakness. It's easy for God to get the glory if we lack the skills and experience to serve in a role God called us to, and God works through us to bring incredible impact. I saw this happen when Elizabeth was called by God to serve in a leadership position in a ministry to young moms. She had no leadership experience outside the home, but she had great impact as a leader because she sought God's wisdom and guidance to work through her, and I saw God give her the spiritual gift of leadership for this role.

I find myself feeling frustrated when I continue to hear the message in church that God wants to work through our weakness. To get us to step up we hear, "God doesn't want your ability. He wants your availability." Yes, God does want to work through our weakness if it fits the purpose He has for us. One of the most well-known biblical examples is Gideon (see Judges 6–8). But this is a *partial* truth. The belief that God works only through our weaknesses can create a mindset, implying God uses us only when we're not deploying our strengths and talents. Is this good stewardship of our abilities and how God designed each of us? This mindset can also lead us to believing God works through our weaknesses for His purposes, while our strengths only matter in everyday life.

According to Mark Legg, "God grants each of us, his image bearers, natural gifts to steward. When we follow Jesus as Lord, we submit those varied blessings, like intelligence, money, influence, public speaking, and charisma, to him. The Holy Spirit empowers us to produce works, or fruit, for God's glory."[20]

The Bible gives us many examples of God working through someone's strengths in matters that impacted others in the cultures where they lived. Joseph was recognized for his great insight and management skills, and God placed him in Pharoah's administration to save Egypt and his family from severe famine (Gen. 41–47). Daniel was highly educated and understood matters of importance to the kings of Babylon. God used Daniel's platform in the king's court to speak to the kings of Babylon (Book of Daniel). Paul was a highly trained Pharisee with great intellect, and God worked through him to bring the message of Jesus to various cultures throughout the Roman Empire (Acts 13–28).

Tim Tebow, the Heisman Trophy-winning quarterback from the University of Florida, had incredible talent. Tim knew God gave him the platform of football to reach others for the Kingdom. Watching Tim play, it was clear he was gifted with great talent that he developed into a strength, but he demonstrated his dependence on God by giving Him the glory. His humility was a great witness to many young talented football players that loved Jesus and loved playing football, letting God use their strengths and their platform to advance His kingdom. His athletic career has ended, and Tim now has a foundation[21] that is his platform where God uses him to impact the lives of the world's most vulnerable people.

Scottie Scheffler is the world's number one golfer at the time of this writing. Golf is the platform where God called him for his kingdom assignment. After winning the Masters championship for the second time, he told interviewers, "I believe in Jesus. Ultimately, I think that's what defines me most. . . . I've been called to come out here, do my best to compete, and glorify God. That's pretty much it."[22] He added, "Winning this golf tournament does not change my identity. My identity is secure, and I cannot emphasize that enough."[23] Scottie's God-given talent for golf has given him a platform and a purpose, allowing him to help others hear what it's like to place God ahead of success.

When operating from a point of strength doing what God is calling us to do, there is something we need to watch out for. When it's easy, we may be tempted to coast a little and not push harder. We can become self-reliant because we don't feel the need for God's strength and guidance. Or we might play it safe and avoid taking a risk. What would God do through us if we go beyond our comfort zone and stretch for God-given goals and dreams we know are beyond our reach, realizing that we need God to be successful? We honor God by depending on Him and doing more than we are capable of, to the glory of God. Jesus said, "Let your light shine before others, so that they may see your good works and give glory to your Father in heaven" (Matt. 5:16 ESV). We must ask God to show us what He wants us to do—what bold outcome He wants us to pursue.

Have you ever taken the time to identify the unique combination of strengths and abilities you possess that can propel you through doing something that others typically struggle to do? It's important to really know yourself. Who you are. How God designed you. Your unique ability. Living life and letting it come out of who you are makes it more impactful, more enjoyable, and less stressful because it feels more natural living that way. You're operating in your sweet spot. And if you continue learning and growing, living this way will become more fun, more impactful, more enjoyable, and less stressful.

As you pivot from one role and one platform to another, you feel more confident that God is working through you and having an impact even though you can't always point to a tangible outcome. I know it because God has done that through me over the last fifteen years—it just gets better each year. I have also watched God do it in the lives of many people I have walked alongside as a coach.

🔑 KEY EXERCISE

Go through each of these key parts of who you are and create a list of characteristics for each one:

- *Your talents and abilities*

- *Your strengths (these are talents and abilities that you have successfully relied on)*

- *Your spiritual gifts*

- *Your core values*

- *Your experience*

- *Your personality*

Ask those who know you well to add to the list you have created. They will see things that may not be obvious to you.

Blessed with financial abundance

We often think of our financial resources as separate from our talents and strengths when it comes to serving others. But the same principles of purpose and stewardship you've explored throughout this book apply to both. Whether God is prompting you to use your **time and abilities** or your **financial resources**, the only difference is in how each is put into action.

Possessing the capacity to be generous financially is a special opportunity that requires intentionality and some strategic thinking. I've coached some and known many others that recognized God has called them to invest their treasure in works that advance God's kingdom by helping spread the gospel, rescue and restore others, and enable human flourishing. Rather than waiting to give assets after they pass away, they actively seek ways to strategically invest now in ministries and ventures that are having significant impact.

Jami and Clint Kaeb saw that one of their key purposes was to pass along to their children the legacy of generosity that Jami got from her dad. In their video story on the Generous Giving website, Jami shares that her dad's dream was to make a lot of money through his business and retire at forty. She says, "God did a radical thing in his heart and really gave him a whole new perspective where he sold the business and gave pretty much all of the money to start ministry."[24]

To free themselves to become more generous, Clint and Jami decided to cap what they would live on at $150,000 for their family with eight children and give away any excess from their family business. Jami says that in the first year this decision "provided us the opportunity to . . . give away $100,000, which was more than triple the amount we had ever given in a year."[25]

The Kaeb's desired outcome from passing along the legacy of generosity was to help their children, as Jami says, "understand we are all vessels." Jami says to their children, "Give generously, receive deeply. . . . Don't hold onto it. Give it back out."[26]

I've been blessed with the opportunity to run a private charitable foundation for over ten years. Doing it well is so much more than sitting down and writing a few big checks. And the joy that comes from being able to come alongside ministries that God is working through to accomplish much is beyond what I could have imagined.

If you believe God has a purpose for you to serve through deploying your financial resources, there are several organizations I have collaborated with that can help explore the best way to do it:

- Ministries dedicated to helping people give strategically:
  - National Christian Foundation[27]
  - Waterstone[28]
  - Orchard Alliance[29]

- Kingdom Advisors is an organization of financial professionals committed to providing principled, competent, biblically sound financial advice.[30]

- Faith Driven Investor is a movement dedicated to helping Christ-following investors believe that God owns it all and that He cares deeply about the how, where, and why behind our investment strategies.[31]

Are you obedient and teachable when God calls?

As we see in the gospels, the four fishermen Jesus called said yes to being his disciples. Both "James and John left their boat and nets, the hired men (Mark 1:20), and their father"[32] to follow Jesus. Peter was not only a fisherman; he also "had a home, a wife, and a mother-in-law in Capernaum"[33] that he left to follow Jesus. "If we obey His word and will, God will guide us" to do what He wants us to do.[34]

These four fishermen were not at first prepared to go out and disciple others. They had a teachable spirit, learning from Jesus and following his leadership. "I will make you fishers of men," Jesus promised (Matt. 4:19).[35]

God may also call you to a role when you don't feel qualified. Elizabeth never served in a leadership position, but she knew God called her and was obedient in response. She thrived because she was teachable and God poured into her, equipping her for significant impact. Don't dismiss an opportunity because you don't feel prepared for it. Will you be obedient and trust Him?

Obedience usually has a cost. It probably won't require leaving your family behind to go on the mission field like Jesus's disciples did but may require going beyond your comfort zone and being available at inconvenient times. The sense of fulfillment will be more than worth the cost.

🔑 KEY EXERCISE

Where do you feel called to live out one of the purposes in your life, but don't feel fully prepared? What is missing? What will you do to get prepared? What is holding you back from pursuing one of the purposes God has for you, letting Him use you there? How will you address this?

Chapter 9

Put It All Together

If you've ever taken a long road trip, you know there is much that needs to be planned before the journey begins. Key elements must be considered for a successful journey. What is the purpose of the journey? Is it to be sure you get to see certain sites within a given time frame, or to get off the main roads and check out life in small towns as you go with no set schedule? Who do you want to travel with and who will you visit while on your trip? Will you determine your route in advance, or let the route emerge as you take your journey? Will you stay in hotels and with friends as you go, or travel in an RV and stay at campgrounds?

Living a fulfilling life journey full of deep joy and meaning also needs planning and includes all the following components:

    A.   your platforms and your roles on each platform

    B.   living out your purpose on each platform

    C.   focused on the important people in your life

    D.   working out of your unique design

Each of the components above are interconnected. Together they are part of your unique journey that is a purpose-driven fulfilling life pursuing God-directed outcomes.

The easiest way to plan your journey for your current or emerging season of life is to approach putting everything together in the above order. But you won't finish working through A before you start to work on B, B before C, or C before D.

Earlier I mentioned Rick, a retired attorney that I had the privilege to coach. One of Rick's key platforms is his extended family. As a grandfather entering a new season of life, his heartfelt desire is for his grandchildren to recognize God's presence in everyday life and trust in His goodness. Living just a few houses away, Rick often walked or drove his grandkids to and from their neighborhood school. Along the way, he would point out glimpses of God in simple elements of nature, offering age-appropriate insights that helped them connect with their Creator through the world around them.

This rhythm brought deep fulfillment to Rick. However, as his grandchildren grew older, he realized that his approach needed to evolve. While his role as a grandfather—and his platform of extended family—remained the same, the new season of life called for a fresh way to live out his purpose and continue influencing his grandkids meaningfully.

Another one of Rick's desired outcomes is to help others become followers of Jesus. One of his platforms is a small group that meets regularly. As a facilitator, his purpose is to provide a safe place for honest dialogue, helping attendees wrestle with the hard questions and better understand what it means to follow Jesus.

These are just two of Rick's desired outcomes, platforms and roles. Rick may be focused on one purpose and role, then focused on his other purpose and role. Rick is not simply "living two lives" at the same time, jumping from one to the other (and other roles and platforms as well) throughout the day or the week. Rick is serving in each role from who Rick is—his unique design. He is doing what he loves doing in different ways, based on the role Rick is focused on at that moment.

I also was a coach for Joe, a highly successful wealth advisor who serves his clients through a biblical lens. Alongside managing their financial well-being, Joe is deeply committed to helping people discover the joy of greater generosity. He refers to himself as a "Chief Generosity Encourager."

Joe hasn't stepped away from his platform as a wealth advisor; instead, he has expanded it. Drawing on his training and experience in major giving, he has embraced a dual purpose of providing financial guidance while inspiring clients to be more open-handed with their resources. Within his advisory practice, Joe operates in two complementary roles: trusted financial advisor and generosity coach. Depending on the moment and the client's needs, he skillfully shifts between these roles to fulfill his broader purpose.

Bob recently retired from a successful career as an executive at a large regional bank. About ten years before his retirement, as I was coaching Bob, he sensed a clear calling from God to invest in men as a mentor, discipler, and leadership coach. He began meeting with colleagues at the bank and men from his church, quickly earning a reputation for helping them grow as leaders, husbands, and fathers.

Over time, Bob was invited to coach leaders across the bank and within the broader business community. For the last decade of his career, he juggled two roles—bank officer and coach. Now fully retired from banking, Bob is dedicating himself to his passion: helping men thrive in leadership and family life. He's building a coaching business rooted in the platform he began over a decade ago.

Scottie Scheffler is at the time of this writing the world's number one golfer. His platform of golf will last as he continues to win, then it will wane. With the awareness that his platform of golf is for a season, right before playing in the British Open (which he won), Doug Ferguson reported in the Associated Press what Scottie said: "Is it great to be able to win tournaments and to accomplish the things I have in the game of golf? Yeah, it brings tears to my eyes just to think about because I've literally worked my entire life to be good at this sport. . . . But at the end of the day, I'm not out here to inspire the next generation of golfers. I'm not out here to inspire someone to be the best player in the world because what's the point? This is not a fulfilling life. It's fulfilling from the sense of accomplishment, but it's not fulfilling from a sense of the deepest places of your heart."[36]

Doug Ferguson, reflecting on Scottie's comments and other things he heard previously, says, "Scheffler is grounded in his faith, in a simple family life with a wife he has been with since high school, a 15-month-old son, three sisters and friends that are not part of the tour community. . . . He often says golf doesn't define him as a person, and he said if it reached a point where the sport ever affected life at home, 'that's going to be the last day that I play out here for a living.'"[37]

Processing the context of what Scottie is saying, golf isn't his only platform nor his most important platform. Golf is also not where he looks for his sense of fulfillment. He does know his purpose on the platform of golf, to glorify God. He also affirms that God, his family, and his friends are all more important platforms than golf.

🔑 KEY EXERCISE

Go back and look at what you wrote down for "What if everything turned out as you hoped?" These are the elements of your fulfilling life. Reviewing what you wrote, make changes as needed to better reflect how you would describe a fulfilling life of purpose. Who do you want to focus on? What are the platforms on which this can happen? Next, write a clear description of your desired outcome for at least one or two of the God-given purposes you believe God has for you. As a good starting point, look at the elements of your fulfilling life, combined with what you hope to accomplish. With the above examples of what others have done, what inspires you? What would make you want to get up every morning and get going? How would you determine your priorities for the roles God has for you on the platforms where He wants to use you?

Chapter 10

Implement Your Plans

If you have planned for a long multi-day road trip, you know of course that if you never depart you will never reach your destination. Following a roadmap or a GPS app on your phone, you get started and keep moving one day at a time until you have arrived at your destination.

Whenever God is giving us a purpose, we should also seek His will for a God-inspired desired outcome—like a destination on a long road trip. The desired outcome presents something to work toward, and we can create a plan and action steps to move us toward what we want to accomplish. Of course—different from a destination on a road trip—the outcome from our planned efforts isn't guaranteed. This is where I will make plans based on the desired outcome but must learn to trust God for the results. I need to remain flexible and adaptable with my plans as God reveals new information. I also need to be intentional without trying to always control what happens along the way, or the outcome.

Jesus makes it clear that God wants to use us. In John 14:12–14, Jesus gives us this promise, "Very truly I tell you, whoever believes in me will do the works I have been doing, and they will do even greater things than these, because I am going to the Father. And I will do whatever you ask in my name, so that the Father may be glorified in the Son. You may ask me for anything in my name, and I will do it" (NIV). Our role may seem minimal, but Jesus used a boy's five loaves and two fishes to feed five thousand people (see John 6:1–13). As the feeding of the five thousand illustrates, God strategically using us can bring great impact.

As was mentioned previously in chapter six about purpose, God will likely have more than one purpose for you—perhaps a different purpose on each of your platforms. Purpose is what motivates you to get going. Take a few minutes to think about three to five of your platforms and your purpose there. What would be a God-inspired desired outcome for your purpose on each platform? Be bold. Don't allow yourself to limit what God may want to do.

At Halftime, we created a tool called a roadmap where someone writes three to five purposes to focus on. After writing out a God-inspired desired outcome for each purpose, action steps are established and added. Because everyday life brings opportunities, challenges, and distractions, the roadmap keeps us focused on what we have decided is a priority. Every sixty to ninety days we update our roadmap, reflecting progress made and possible changes in priorities.

What is keeping you from pursuing the purposes God is giving you?

Looking at what you want to accomplish, are you feeling some uncertainty that it can be done? What is behind that? Time constraints? Financial constraints? Does it seem impossible?

Below are some assumptions I've observed in me and others that can become limiting beliefs.

The limiting belief that we can control the outcome

The world in which we live measures success by results. I have set many goals with expected results, and if the results I was working toward were not accomplished, I felt like a failure. I had to learn that if what I was pursuing is from God, I had to also trust what He will do. As God directs us, our role is to be faithful in doing what we can do and remember that we don't control the outcomes. God may not bring the results we hoped for, but the results God brings are always good.

The limiting belief that we cannot make a difference

We hear inspiring stories of what others have done, and we think, *I can't do what they did. I don't have their abilities or access to a platform like they do.* This can cause us to never start because we are thinking, *What's the point? God won't use me like that.* Or we get going with what God called us to do and experience a setback, and we think, *This must not be what God was calling me to do.* I had to learn that pursuing something worthwhile, especially for God, will not be as easy as others can make it sound when they tell their stories of what God did. After a setback, I had to seek confirmation from God whether I was doing what He called me to do, then ask God to show we what to do next and get going again.

The limiting belief that it's too risky

The older I get, the less I'm willing to take risk. I am unable to see how I can do it, so why start? Granted, some of that is wisdom, but there is also the risk of playing it too safe. I start thinking about "what if this happens or that happens?," which brings anxiety and fear. Sometimes it is necessary to forget about the how and just think, what if God were to do this through me? I must also identify the risks I am seeing in my mind creating fear and keeping me from proceeding. Obvious risks may be possible, like financial loss or getting hurt physically. Is it as risky as I am making it in my mind? A less obvious risk could be a sense of shame if I don't succeed. Another risk is looking incompetent until I get better at doing something. Once I've identified the risks holding me back, I ask God to help me work through what risks are worth taking, and what risks are not. Can I reduce some of the risk with reasonable effort? At some point I must accept the risk and proceed with what God is calling me to do, trusting God to guide me toward the outcome.

The limiting belief that we don't have time

If it seems like I have too much to do and feel stressed, I can't experience the joy and fulfillment that comes from doing what God has as His purpose for me. Realizing this, I pause and consider what I am committed to. What is consuming my days? Is it time for some necessary endings? Do I need to intentionally abandon some things no longer useful or no longer important? Do I have possessions in my life taking time and money to maintain, but their usefulness has passed? Are there things I'm doing that others like to do or could do for me?

Have I unconsciously let someone else set my agenda, not in big ways, but in little ways resulting in a noticeable impact on my time? We can look through social media or something similar without realizing how much time has passed. Scrolling through emails, looking at promotions and newsletters can become a time waster. Every website has popups designed to entice me to stop what I'm doing and pursue what was suddenly thrown in front of my face. Searching on Amazon for the best option before buying something can become time consuming if not careful.

What is it that may be taking more of your time than you realize and has become an unintended habit? Watching sports? 24/7 TV news? Reality TV? YouTube videos? Old movies? Scrolling Facebook or TikTok? Browsing on Amazon? If this has become subconscious activity, does it require breaking the habit by stopping cold turkey for a few days or weeks? If not stopping altogether, do you need to limit the time engaging in it?

Technological advances have greatly improved modern life, but I'm noticing that increasingly my technology applications regularly fail to work, requiring me to stop and pursue how to fix it. One app doing this isn't usually a big deal, but when it's several in a day, it adds up. The solution for nonperforming technology isn't as easy to solve since that is out of my control. But what I can do is resist the temptation to automate through technology more of my daily activities and conveniences, with the presumed belief that this will always make my life better, saving me time and improving efficiency. I've started to choose a different path. Increasingly, I just let a failed application wait to be corrected later when it is more convenient for me to address it, and sometimes it self-corrects. With greater self-awareness I'm striving to consciously choose what I will do with my time rather than passively let things happen. I also regularly ask for God's help to discern what is beyond my control and what is worthy of addressing, gaining back wasted time.

Ask yourself (and ask your spouse if you have the courage), how hard are you going every day? Are you trying to do too much? Do you say you are trusting God, but living like it all depends on you? Psalm 127:1–2 says, "Unless the Lord builds a house, the work of the builders is wasted. Unless the Lord protects a city, guarding it with sentries will do no good. It is useless for you to work so hard from early morning until late at night, anxiously working for food to eat; for God gives rest to his loved ones" (NLT).

Based on your God-given purposes, what action steps will you take to get things moving and keep them moving?

It's easy to go with the flow and hope something significant occurs, or tell myself I will get started when or after this or that happens. Action steps get us moving. They put our intentions into motion, are very practical, and are something we can commit to do now, this week, and within the next sixty to ninety days.

Using the long road trip example, unless we depart we will never get there. Once we depart we must adapt. A different route than planned may be necessary, or as happened to us on one trip, we had to change a destination because of a fire the day before we planned to visit.

Just like the steps you take when embarking on a road trip, your action steps need to be basic, sequential, and adaptable as new information is discovered. We intuitively know these things, but sometimes we still get stuck. We don't have to see every step from start to finish to get started, as each next step will likely become intuitive. But we must start moving forward.

Keep going, a step at a time, until you have accomplished what God is guiding you to do. Two verses in Proverbs illustrate how to approach this. "Commit to the Lord whatever you do, and he will establish your plans" (Prov. 16:3 NIV). "In their hearts humans plan their course, but the Lord establishes their steps" (v. 9).

What will you do to get started? When will you do it?

Examples of Purpose in Action

Below are two real-life examples from people I've coached, showing how clarity about purpose, desired outcomes, and platforms can guide intentional living.

Example 1: A Grandfather Investing in His Grandchildren

Purpose: Encourage grandchildren to know Jesus and build a vibrant relationship with Him.

Desired Outcome: Grandchildren regularly talk about how they seek God's guidance, trust Him in their struggles, and depend on Him in sports and other activities.

Platform: Family

Role: Grandfather

Important People: Grandchildren

Action Plan:

1. Take each grandchild out for breakfast once a month.

2. Share what God is currently teaching and showing me.

3. Be transparent about my own struggles, how I seek God's direction, and how I trust Him with outcomes.

4. Ask about their lives and what's on their hearts.

5. Ask how I can pray for them and follow up on those prayers.

Example 2: A Business Owner Living His Faith at Work

Purpose: Point others to Jesus as their Savior and as their source of strength and comfort.

Desired Outcome: Those facing struggles begin trusting Jesus in their daily lives.

Platform: Business

Role: Owner and Manager

Important People: Employees, customers, and suppliers

Action Plan:

1. Be open about my faith in Jesus in natural, authentic ways.

2. Get to know customers, employees, and suppliers personally by:
   o Asking about their families, weekends, and hobbies.

3. Listen carefully for areas of struggle or concern.

4. Offer to pray for them when appropriate.

5. Look for tangible ways to help when needs arise.

🔑 KEY EXERCISE

Think about your platforms. Are you clear on your desired outcome for living out at least one or two of your God-given purposes on those platforms? If not, go back and write that out first. With your desired outcomes in mind, what are basic measurable action steps you can take to get started? When will you start? Write it down and refer to it regularly to keep it fresh in your mind.

Can you trust God's timing?

One of the challenges of pursuing God's purpose is to get in sync with God's timing. We can develop our plans and action steps and proceed, then nothing seems to happen. This can bring doubt. Did I not hear God correctly? Did I do something wrong?

Of course, we need to ask God to reveal anything He wants to change, making sure we are hearing Him correctly. And we need to ask God for affirmation and encouragement. Proverbs 3:5–6 says, "Trust in the Lord with all your heart; do not depend on your own understanding. Seek his will in all you do, and he will show you which path to take" (NLT).

If we are stuck or unsure what to do, James 1:5–7 tells us that if we ask God for wisdom, He will give it generously:

> If any of you lacks wisdom, you should ask God, who gives generously to all without finding fault, and it will be given to you. But when you ask, you must believe and not doubt, because the one who doubts is like a

wave of the sea, blown and tossed by the wind. That person should not expect to receive anything from the Lord. (NIV)

We may be doing exactly as God wants us to do, even though it may not seem like it. I heard Jim Vandermeer, senior pastor of Woodland Park Community Church, comment in his message on Psalm 1 that it is not easy to keep trying and see no results, especially if we are a high achiever who gets things done.[38] Psalm 1 tells us that we will yield fruit in season, meaning God determines when the results will come and how productive they will be.

When nothing seems to be happening and you can't get anything started, maybe God is calling you to shift into neutral and be totally open to hearing what God wants you to know, how God wants to use you, and when He wants to use you. As Terry Looper talks about in his book *Sacred Pace*, "In God's sovereign timing—His Spirit leads us to a sacred place: the center of God's will. Our part is to wait on the Lord with our eyes, ears, and hearts wide open."[39] Psalm 37:7 says, "Be still before the Lord and wait patiently for him; do not fret when people succeed in their ways, when they carry out their wicked schemes" (NIV).

In the late 1980s I felt certain that God was calling me to become a wealth advisor, providing advice and counsel with a biblical mindset. With my background and training as a CPA, I started working toward building a business that could provide for our family. To cover living expenses, I accepted a faculty position at a local university that provided flexibility in my schedule. I planned to be there for three to five years.

When we believe God is calling us to something we expect doors to open and opportunities to emerge that confirm what we heard from God. I tried many things that produced little fruit.

I started having doubts God wanted to use me as a biblically aligned wealth advisor. I lost count of the number of times I was so discouraged I wanted to quit, but God wouldn't let the dream die. Each time I learned something wasn't working, God showed me a new idea. I kept my risk of financial commitment low in case it didn't work out until I saw some traction. Finally, God brought me into a partnership with two like-minded friends that were father and son, Ray and Rob West, and together we built a business that was exactly what God was calling me to do. Three to five years to reach my goal turned into fifteen years. We later sold our company to Ronald Blue & Co. (now BlueTrust), where I continued to serve as a wealth advisor for many more years.

I'll never fully understand why it took so long to reach the goal God led me to set. But a blessing that came out of the struggle was I learned a lot about trusting God and His timing when things didn't make sense and I was discouraged and despondent.

In another circumstance, God's timing was much quicker than we anticipated. When God made it clear He wanted us to move to Colorado from South Florida, we couldn't foresee how we could make it happen. In 2011, we made the decision to move to Colorado and set a goal for 2020, the year our son was retiring from the Army and moving to Colorado. God led us to start looking for a house to buy in Colorado in 2013. Since we didn't feel any urgency, we decided to create a list of things we wanted in a house, then start looking. Within a few weeks, God led us to a house that was exactly what we were looking for. Although we were not where we planned to be financially before proceeding, we felt God guiding us to buy it.

This was 2013 and we still didn't expect to move to Colorado until 2020. We rented out our Colorado home as a vacation rental with a lot of success. But through a chain of events, God opened doors in rapid and amazing ways. In 2014, God led me to leave my position with Ronald Blue & Co to co-found a charitable foundation and continue coaching for Halftime. That provided the opportunity to move to Colorado in 2014, six years ahead of our goal. God revealed the reason for His timing after getting there, which was to use both me and Elizabeth in two different ministries where we had leadership roles.

When you become confident that what you're pursuing is what God is leading you to do, can you trust God's timing? What will you do when you start feeling doubt about God's purpose for you?

Who will hold you accountable?

We have all let it happen. We're motivated and have good intentions to take action, then everyday life hits and we get caught up in solving problems and meeting personal needs. The plans to do what God called us to do gets pushed aside.

We may conclude we can't do it because of other demands and give up. Unless we push through these setbacks and distractions, the change we hoped for and the joy and fulfillment we are seeking will never come.

Who can you ask to encourage you, to challenge you? Who will follow up with you if you haven't reached out to report how you are progressing?

Chapter 11

Eighteen Months from Now

Go back and look at what you wrote down in Chapter 3 that describes "what if everything turned out as you hoped?" Take a few minutes and invite God to give you a vision of your future eighteen months from now. With another look at what you wrote, you might feel led to make some changes. Go ahead. Including changes you made, what does the destination look like?

Will you reach this destination in eighteen months? Probably not perfectly. We are told we can't control the future. In many ways that is true, but we can shape how we approach what the future brings. If we depend on God, He will empower us to take the steps to move toward the destination.

Whether the destination you reach is exactly how you pictured it or some version of that, the journey is the adventure. Your journey will be exhilarating, rewarding, sometimes a little scary. The journey will also include obstacles, detours, delays, and unexpected experiences that exceed expectations. Invite God to be your guide and companion.

With the destination in your mind, embrace the journey. Be intentional. Establish action steps then take them, adjusting as the journey unfolds. When you get off course, regroup and start again. When you get stopped and can't go any further, wait on God to show you what to do next when He is ready for you to proceed.

What happens is in God's hands as you take your journey. Trust Him. Thank Him for the daily experiences. Make note of even the small blessings God brings into your life every day as you are being used by God. And don't give up.

Chapter 12

How Can I Know If I Need a Coach?

I hope this book has challenged you, encouraged you, and stirred you to action. If so, I am glad God used me in this way. But if what I wrote spoke to you and challenged you, but you are either not sure where to start, or you got started and now you are stuck?

As a Halftime coach,[40] I've had the privilege of being used by God to come alongside many people and serve as their guide. I was able to help them get clear about how God wants to use them, get free so they can proceed, then get going.

How can you know if you need a coach? Let's revisit the list from Chapter 1—the things people shared when they first came to Halftime for coaching. Where do you see yourself in the following statements?

- A significant season of life has come to an end, and I'm not sure what I want to do in this emerging new season.

- I'm trying to find ways to be more intentional in how I reflect Jesus in my business/work, or in my family.

- I've been very successful in my career, but it no longer brings the satisfaction it once did.

- I've been successful, but some important relationships have not received appropriate attention, and I am not sure how to reengage with them.

- I no longer enjoy my work (or business) like I once did, but this is who I am. I don't know who I would be if I retired (or sold my business).

- I'm experiencing burnout and realize I need a reset but not sure how I want to reposition myself going forward.

- I'm good at what I do and compensated well, but I want to have more meaningful impact in my work.

- I don't feel like Jesus is working through me, but I'm not sure what to do so God can use me more effectively.

- I've been serving God, but I also feel spiritually dry.

- It feels like I'm doing all the right things, but I don't know why I'm not seeing the results.

- I've been trying to transition into a new purpose-driven life but seem to be stuck and don't know how to get going.

If you read this book and any of the above speaks to you, do you know what to do to get started? If so, perhaps you don't need a coach to come alongside and guide you. But if you feel uncertain what to do, not sure how to start, or you started and now you are stuck, you may benefit from coaching.

To let God use you in ways that are more consistent and intentional than occasionally praying for someone, serving, or sharing the gospel, you must be willing to go through a wilderness period. In the wilderness God may seem silent. Uncertainty is high, nothing seems to be happening, or you can't get something started. Self-confidence, doubt and discouragement can surface. If you persevere you will get through it, but it can be challenging. This is when having a coach can be most valuable. Much clarity can emerge when someone else will listen to you think your confusion out loud and reflect to you what they're hearing. Having been where you are now and gotten through it, a coach's questions can provide breakthroughs.

Something else is critical—the desire to do something now. How many of us read a book or heard a speaker that stirred us, and we think "Someday I'll . . ."? If the feeling is nothing more than "Someday I'll . . .," you are not ready to get started.

But on the other hand, if you can't stop thinking about it and your mind wanders to considering ways to do what I talk about in this book, you are ready to get going now. If you are feeling a sense of restlessness and it won't go away, you are ready to get started now. If this is you, will you put into practice what you read in this book, or would having a coach help you get started?

I'm glad to offer a one-hour complimentary coaching call at no charge. My purpose on that call is to serve you and help you. If you express any interest in exploring coaching beyond this complimentary call, I'll help you discern if you would benefit from more coaching, and if you're willing to invest the time to get the full value from coaching. Coaching isn't for everyone, and I haven't served you or me well if we start coaching and you're not ready to do what is needed for it to help you. If you're not ready for coaching now, it's okay. Many are not ready now but are ready later.

If you'd like to schedule a complimentary one-hour coaching session at no charge to explore anything you read in this book, reach out to me at: jim@nextseasonnavigator.com

If you would like to learn more about all we do at Halftime to help followers of Jesus get clear, get free and get going, go to https://halftime.org

Endnotes

1   Rick Warren, *The Purpose-Driven Life* (Zondervan, 2002), 31.

2   Warren, *The Purpose-Driven Life*, 32.

3   Ken Blanchard, foreword to Bob Buford, *Finishing Well: The Adventure of Life Beyond Halftime* (Zondervan, 2011), xi.

4   Blanchard, *Finishing Well*, xvii.

5   HalftimeOnDemand, "Becoming Chief Life Officer [Pete Chambers]," April 4, 2022, https://www.youtube.com/watch?v=VC8yj2xzUiM.

6   Jim Denison, "How to Be Strategic With Your Life," Denison Forum, August 13, 2024, https://www.denisonforum.org/church-leadership/how-to-be-strategic-with-your-life/.

7   https://halftime.org/coaches/.

8   https://halftime.org/coaches/.

9   https://faithdrivenentrepreneur.org.

10   Pete Ochs, "Jailhouse Business of Generosity," Faith Driven Entrepreneur, https://faithdrivenentrepreneur.subspla.sh/6mn885n.

11   Ochs, "Jailhouse Business of Generosity."

12   Ochs, "Jailhouse Business of Generosity."

13   Terry Looper and Kris Bearss, *Sacred Pace: Four Steps to Hearing God and Aligning Yourself with His Will* (Thomas Nelson, 2019), 24–25. Kindle.

14   https://halftime.org/.

15   Denison, "How to be Strategic With Your Life."

16   HalftimeOnDemand, "Becoming Chief Life Officer [Pete Chambers]."

17   Lloyd and Linda Reeb, *Halftime for Couples: Building a Second Half of Impact and Adventure Together* (Halftime Institute, 2012).

18   https://halftime.org/.

19   https://halftime.org/.

20   Mark Legg, "Is Young Hoon Kim the "World's Smartest Man" and a Christian?," Denison Forum, September 23, 2025, https://www.denisonforum.org/current-events/is-younghoon-kim-the-worlds-smartest-man-and-a-christian/.

21   https://timtebowfoundation.org.

22   Jim Denison, "Scottie Scheffler After His Masters Triumph," Denison Forum, April 16, 2024, https://www.denisonforum.org/daily-article/scottie-scheffler-after-his-masters-triumph/.

23   Denison, "Scottie Scheffler After His Masters Triumph."

24   "Jami and Clint Kaeb," Generous Giving, https://generousgiving.org/jami-and-clint-kaeb/.

25   "Jami and Clint Kaeb."

26   "Jami and Clint Kaeb."

27   https://www.ncfgiving.com.

28   https://waterstone.org.

29 https://orchardalliance.org.

30 https://kingdomadvisors.com/find-a-cka.

31 https://faithdriveninvestor.org/mission-and-vision/.

32 https://faithdriveninvestor.org/mission-and-vision/.

33 https://faithdriveninvestor.org/mission-and-vision/.

34 https://faithdriveninvestor.org/mission-and-vision/.

35 Denison, "How to Be Strategic With Your Life."

36 Doug Ferguson, "Scottie Scheffler is chasing the claret jug at the British Open and searching for what it all means," Associated Press, July 15, 2025, https://apnews.com/article/scottie-scheffler-british-open-royal-portrush-1ae549fd5b0fd51663ed756784bf2bca.

37 Ferguson, "Scottie Scheffler is chasing the claret jug at the British Open and searching for what it all means."

38 Jim Vandermeer, "The Blessed Man, Psalm 1" (sermon, Woodland Park Community Church, July 13, 2025).

39 Looper and Bearss, *Sacred Pace*, 33–34. Kindle.

40 https://halftime.org/coaches/.

About the Author

Jim Dean calls himself a next season navigator. He is a leadership coach with Halftime and co-founded the John Stiger Ferry Charitable Foundation, where he serves as president and board chairman. Since 2013, Jim has been serving as a navigator for high-capacity leaders, helping them gain clarity around God's unique calling for their lives, overcome distractions, and take meaningful steps toward their purpose.

With over four decades of experience across finance, business, nonprofits, trusts and estates, and legacy development, Jim brings a broad and seasoned perspective to his coaching. He has launched businesses and nonprofits, advised corporate executives and business owners, and supported families in navigating purpose and legacy. A former wealth advisor with Ronald Blue & Co. (now Blue Trust), Jim is known for his ability to distill complexity into clear direction and actionable strategy.

Jim and his wife, Elizabeth, live in a peaceful Central Florida community. They enjoy pickleball, golf, and building memories with their two children and their spouses and three grandchildren.

Jim can be reached at jim@nextseasonnavigator.com.